M000240214

HER STAGE NAME IS "TINA TURNER," A NAME GIVEN TO HER BY HER LATE – AND VIOLENT – HUSBAND, IKE TURNER.

DURING AN INTERVIEW WITH *SPIN* MAGAZINE IN 1985, IKE SAID:

"YEAH, I HIT HER, BUT I DIDN'T HIT HER MORE THAN THE AVERAGE GUY BEATS HIS WIFE.

"THE TRUTH IS, OUR LIFE WAS NO DIFFERENT FROM THE GUY NEXT DOOR'S. IT'S BEEN EXAGGERATED.

"PEOPLE BUY BAD NEWS, DIRTY NEWS. IF SHE SAYS I ABUSED HER, MAYBE I DID."

TINA TOOK THE NAME IKE GAVE HER, BUT SHE DIDN'T ALLOW IKE'S ACTIONS, SENSATIONALIZED OR NOT, TO DEFINE HER.

HER STORY ISN'T ABOUT ABUSE.

IT'S ABOUT SURVIVING.

AND THRIVING.

TINA WAS BORN ANNA MAE BULLOCK ON NOVEMBER 26, 1939, IN NUTBUSH, TENNESSEE, A SMALL TOWN ABOUT 75 HIGHWAY MILES FROM MEMPHIS.

HER PARENTS, FLOYD AND ZELMA BULLOCK, WORKED AS SHARECROPPERS.

THEY WEREN'T POOR. THAT'S NOT HOW TINA SAW HER CHILDHOOD.

SHE THOUGHT OF HER FAMILY AS "WELL-TO-DO FARMERS."

FLOYD WAS A DEACON IN THE LOCAL CHURCH, WHILE ZELMA WAS A HOMEMAKER. THEY WEREN'T EDUCATED PEOPLE. THEY WORKED THE SOIL AND COBBLED TOGETHER A LIFE AS BEST THEY COULD MANAGE.

"WE HAD FOOD ON THE TABLE. WE JUST DIDN'T HAVE FANCY THINGS LIKE BICYCLES," TINA ONCE TOLD AN INTERVIEWER FOR ROLLING STONE.

STRESS DOES THINGS TO PEOPLE, AND A DARKNESS SETTLED OVER THE BULLOCK HOME, A SPECTER THAT WOULD FOLLOW TINA THROUGH HER FORMATIVE YEARS.

TINA WONDERED IF HER PARENTS EVER LOVED EACH OTHER.

DURING WORLD WAR II, HER FATHER AND MOTHER WORKED IN A DEFENSE FACILITY IN KNOXVILLE, CONTRIBUTING TO THE WAR EFFORT. TINE AND HER TWO OLDER SISTERS, ALLINE AND EVELYN, WERE SEPARATED, AND TINA WAS LEFT IN THE CARE OF HER GRANDPARENTS.

DURING THIS TIME IN HER LIFE, TINA DESCRIBED HERSELF AS INNOCENT, LISTENING TO COUNTRY AND WESTERN MUSIC AND B.B. KING ON HER RADIO.

SHE DIDN'T KNOW ANYTHING ABOUT WHAT IT WAS LIKE TO BE A STAR UNTIL, SHE TOLD OPRAH WINFREY, "THE WHITE PEOPLE ALLOWED US TO COME DOWN AND WATCH THEIR TELEVISION ONCE A WEEK."

THOSE WHITE PEOPLE? THE POINDEXTERS, THE LANDLORDS WHO OWNED THE FARM HER PARENTS WORKED.

AFTER THE WAR, SHE REJOINED HER PARENTS AND ATTENDED FLAGG GROVE ELEMENTARY IN NUTBUSH, WHERE SHE SANG IN LOCAL TALENT SHOWS AND HER CHURCH.

THE SPECTER THAT FOLLOWED TINA'S PARENTS GREW DARKER.

ZELMA LEFT FOR ST. LOUIS WHEN TINA WAS ABOUT ELEVEN YEARS OLD. SHE'D LEFT THE FAMILY BEFORE, BUT FLOYD ALWAYS FOLLOWED HER AND CONVINCED HER TO RETURN.

THIS TIME, TINA KNEW THAT PROMISES AND HONEYED WORDS WOULDN'T MAKE ANY DIFFERENCE.

SO DID FLOYD.

HE LEFT FOR DETROIT TWO YEARS LATER.

LOOK AT THOSE LEGS!

STARDOM ALWAYS SEEMED FAR AWAY TO TINA UNTIL SHE SAW BETTY GRABLE.

MOVIE GALAXY

MAY 15¢

BETTY GRABLE

AMAZING PINUP GIRL

EXTRA GOSSIP PAGES!

WHO IS THAT?

BETTY GRABLE! WHAT, DO YOU LIVE UNDER A ROCK? SHE'S FROM ST. LOUIS, YOU KNOW. IF A GIRL LIKE THAT CAN MAKE IT BIG...

WHAT'S THE FASCINATION?

THERE WAS SOMETHING ABOUT HER WAY. SHE WAS A MIDWESTERN GIRL WHO MADE IT BIG, STARRING IN 42 MOVIES THAT GROSSED MILLIONS.

SHE'S IN PROPORTION, HARRY, SEE? HER LEGS ARE JUST THE RIGHT LENGTH. MINE –

GO ON FOR MILES. I LIKE YOUR LEGS.

STOP IT.

TINA USED TO HATE HER LEGS, THINKING, "WHY DO I LOOK LIKE A LITTLE PONY?"

EXTRA GOSSIP PAGES!

THE WAY GRABLE DRESSED SEEMED JUST RIGHT. SHE KNEW HOW TO USE HER GIFTS TO HER ADVANTAGE. IF SHE COULD DO IT, THEN MAYBE...?

WHEN TINA FIRST SAW HARRY TAYLOR, SHE WAS SMITTEN.

SHE WAS A CHEERLEADER FOR THE BASKETBALL TEAM AT CARVER HIGH SCHOOL IN TENNESSEE WHILE HARRY WAS ON THE TEAM.

WATCHING HIM, SOMETHING STIRRED INSIDE. SHE MADE A POINT TO PAY ATTENTION WHEN HE WAS ON THE COURT.

"IT WAS LOVE AT FIRST SIGHT, AND WHENEVER I SAW HIM, MY HEART STARTED BEATING SO FAST THAT I WAS AFRAID IT WOULD JUMP FROM MY BODY," TINA TOLD AN INTERVIEWER.

SHE ASKED ONE OF THE TEAM TRAINERS TO INTRODUCE THEM.

BUT SHE CHICKENED OUT. SHE WASN'T READY.

EVENTUALLY, THEY'D FIND EACH OTHER AGAIN.

THEY STARTED SLOW.

VERY SLOW.

WHAT?

BUT... YOU DON'T KNOW HOW TO KISS!

I, WELL, I....

IT'S OKAY. HERE.

OPEN YOUR MOUTH A LITTLE. JUST. LIKE...

THE GAME WAS ON.

AFTER HIGH SCHOOL, HARRY JOINED THE AIR FORCE. TINA'S GRANDMOTHER PASSED AWAY. SO, LIKE BETTY GRABLE, SHE MOVED TO ST. LOUIS WITH HER MOTHER.

TIME AND DISTANCE — AND THE ALLURE OF OTHER, MORE IMMEDIATE WOMEN FOR HARRY — DOUSED THE FIRES OF THEIR RELATIONSHIP.

ST. LOUIS WAS A NEW START FOR TINA.

SHE GREW REBELLIOUS AND TOOK TO HANGING OUT IN R & B CLUBS WITH HER SISTER, ALLINE, EVEN THOUGH SHE WASN'T OLD ENOUGH TO GET INTO THE CLUB.

A BARMAID AT CLUB MANHATTAN, ALLINE WAS POPULAR WITH THE MEN.

"MY SISTER WAS BEAUTIFUL. I WAS SKINNY, WITH LONG LEGS, AND NOT ATTRACTIVE. TO TURN A BLACK MAN'S HEAD, YOU HAD TO BE HEAVIER . . . SEXIER LOOKING," TINA TOLD *ROLLING STONE.*

"ALLINE HAD BIG BOOBS, BLACK, BLACK SKIN AND THE SAME FEATURES AS MINE, BUT SMALLER. SHE HAD A LOT OF STYLE. SHE ALWAYS WORE STILETTOS AND BLACK STOCKINGS WITH A SEAM. HER HAIR WAS SOFT, WHILE MY HAIR WAS FULL AND THICK.

"ALLINE WAS SEXY."

HMMM-MMM-MMM... YEAH!

IT WASN'T A SECRET THAT TINA WANTED TO BE A SINGER. IF YOU SAT NEXT TO HER AT CLUB MANHATTAN, YOU COULD HEAR HER HUMMING THE NOTES AND VOCALIZING.

SOMETHING THAT DIDN'T GO UNNOTICED BY THE BAND.

C'MON, LITTLE SISTER. LET'S HEAR IT!

♪♪ HMMM-MMM-MMM... ♪♪ I - WHAT?

AT FIRST, THE KING'S OF RHYTHM, THE BAND WHO PULLED IN THE CROWDS AT THE CLUB, WASN'T SURE ALLINE'S LITTLE SISTER COULD SING. SHE WAS SKINNY AND FRAIL, AND THEY WONDERED IF SHE HAD THE PIPES.

A GIRL NAMED PAT WAS ONE THEY USUALLY PULLED UP ONSTAGE TO SING. THE REASONS, BESIDES THAT SHE COULD SING ALMOST AS WELL AS TINA, WERE EVIDENT.

BUT THAT NIGHT, THINGS CHANGED.

FINE, BUT GIVE ME SOME B.B. KING. MAKE IT MOVE.

YEARS LATER, LITTLE RICHARD DESCRIBED TINA'S STYLE:

"SHE SANG THE BLUES UP-TEMPO - AND THEY CALLED IT ROCK 'N ROLL."

FORGET MARRIAGE.

THANKS, MAN.

ANY... ANYTIME, ANNA MAE. ANY $#%& TIME!

HEY, LEGS! YEAH, YOU!

FORGET CHILDREN.

GIRL, I DIDN'T KNOW YOU COULD SING!

ALLINE BEEN HOLDIN' OUT ON US.

I'M...

IKE TURNER. YEAH, I KNOW. I'M HERE EVERY NIGHT. ANNA MAE.

FORGET LIVING HAPPILY EVER AFTER AS SOMEONE'S WIFE.

THAT WAS GONE. AFTER ALL, HOW COULD ANY OF THAT COMPARE TO THIS?

HOW'D YOU FEEL 'BOUT JOININ' US ONSTAGE MORE OFTEN?

YEAH, SURE, BUT YOU'LL HAVE TO CLEAR IT WITH MY MOM.

YOU'RE... HOW OLD ARE YOU, SUGAR?

SHE DIDN'T FIND HIM ATTRACTIVE. HE WAS SINEW, MUSCLE, AND BONE – ALMOST FERAL IN APPEARANCE. BUT ONSTAGE?

SEVENTEEN. I'M SEVENTEEN.

SEVENTEEN.

HE WAS MAGIC. MAGNETIC. TALENTED.

WHEN THE BAND LOST ITS LEAD SINGER, IKE ASKED TINA TO JOIN THEM. AT FIRST, TINA AND IKE WERE CLOSE FRIENDS, MORE AKIN TO A BROTHER AND A SISTER.

SHE FOUND RAYMOND HILL, THE SAXOPHONIST FOR IKE'S BAND, ATTRACTIVE, BUT SHE WASN'T IN LOVE WITH HIM, AT LEAST, NOT IN THE WAY SHE FELT LOVE WITH HARRY.

WHEN SHE GOT PREGNANT, SHE MOVED IN WITH HIM.

SINGING AS A BACKUP IN THE BAND WAS SOMEWHAT SATISFYING, BUT WITH A CHILD (AN ABORTION WAS OUT OF THE QUESTION FOR TINA) ON THE WAY, SHE THOUGHT SHE'D GO TO SCHOOL AND BECOME A NURSE, GET A JOB, AND HAVE THE BABY.

MAYBE SHE COULD BE A HOMEMAKER AFTER ALL.

BUT THE RELATIONSHIP WAS SHORT-LIVED. IKE TOLD *THE DAILY BEAST* IN 2015:

"IF I REALLY WANTED TO TALK $%&# ABOUT TINA, I COULD. SHE AND HER SAXOPHONE-PLAYER BOYFRIEND WERE LIVING IN MY HOUSE IN EAST ST. LOUIS. HE GOT TINA PREGNANT.

"I'D GET MAD AT HIM, 'CAUSE HE'D MAKE TINA GO DOWNSTAIRS WHILE HE WENT UPSTAIRS TO BALL ANOTHER WOMAN. WHERE DOES SHE COME OFF SOUNDING SO INNOCENT THESE DAYS?"

AFTER BREAKING HIS FOOT, RAYMOND MOVED IN WITH HIS FAMILY, AND TINA RETURNED TO HER MOTHER'S HOUSE.

HER FIRST CHILD WAS BORN WHEN TINA WAS 18.

CRAIG TURNER COMMITTED SUICIDE IN 2018 AT THE AGE OF 59.

TINA TOLD OPRAH WINFREY:

"I'M STILL TRYING TO FIND OUT WHY HE DID IT. MAYBE SOMETHING FROM HIS CHILDHOOD FOLLOWED HIM THROUGH LIFE AND WAS STILL WEIGHING ON HIM, AND HE JUST COULDN'T HANDLE IT ANYMORE. I DON'T KNOW .

"I BELIEVE HIS NEXT LIFE WILL BE EASIER. HE'S IN A GOOD PLACE."

WHEN TINA MOVED TO LEAD SINGER, IKE TREATED HER WELL.

OH, YEAH!

SO HOT!

SING IT, GIRL!

"IKE WENT OUT AND BOUGHT ME A FUR, A DRESS, SOME HIGH-HEELED SHOES. HE GOT MY HAIR ALL DONE UP. I RODE TO WORK IN A PINK CADILLAC. I EVEN GOT MY TEETH FIXED," SAID TINA.

ON THEIR NIGHTS OFF, THEY'D CRUISE TOWN. HE'D TELL HER ABOUT HIS CHILDHOOD, HOW PEOPLE FOUND HIM UNATTRACTIVE AND HOW MUCH IT HURT HIM, SHARING HIS SECRET FEARS.

IKE. I'D NEVER HURT YOU. EVER.

HE WAS FRIENDLY, PUTTING TINA ON A PEDESTAL THAT MADE IT HARD FOR HER TO SEE HIM. AFTER ALL, WHEN YOU'RE ON TOP OF THE WORLD, EVERYTHING ELSE LOOKED SMALL.

HIS ARGUMENTS AND FIGHTS WITH OTHER PEOPLE, SHE ASSUMED, WERE BECAUSE THEY WRONGED HIM. ALL WAS RIGHT BETWEEN THEM. SHE EVEN AGREED TO CHANGE HER NAME.

THE FIRST SIGN OF TROUBLE CAME WHEN TINA TOLD IKE NO FOR THE FIRST TIME.

NO ONE TOLD IKE NO. NO ONE.

CHAPTER 4: PROUD MARY.

HE FIRST STARTED TOUCHING TINA IN THE BACKSEAT OF HIS CAR DURING ONE OF THEIR TALKS. SHE DIDN'T LIKE IT, BUT SHE ALLOWED IT TO HAPPEN OUT OF A SENSE OF LOYALTY TO HIM.

C'MON, IKE! WE'RE JUST TALKING HERE.

OKAY, BUT I CAN'T HELP IT. YOU'RE SO FINE!

THEY RECORDED "A FOOL FOR LOVE" AND SENT IT TO A NEW YORK PRODUCER WHEN THEIR RELATIONSHIP WAS MUDDY AND UNDEFINED.

AFTER A RUN-IN BACKSTAGE, TINA FELT THAT THINGS – THAT IKE – WASN'T RIGHT. SHE DECIDED THE BEST THING TO DO WAS LEAVE THE BAND AND START OVER.

AT HIS HOUSE IN EAST ST. LOUIS, HE BEAT HER WITH A WOODEN SHOE STRETCHER.

OH, YOU WANT TO HURT ME LIKE EVERYONE ELSE, DON'T YA? YEAH, THAT'S WHAT THIS IS.

THE RECORD WAS A HIT. THE BAND WAS RENAMED THE IKE AND TINA TURNER REVUE, RELEASING A STRING OF FOLLOW-UP SINGLES INCLUDING "IT'S GONNA WORK OUT FINE," "POOR FOOL," AND "TRA LA LA LA LA."

IKE AND TINA MARRIED IN TIJUANA, MEXICO, IN 1962. SHE ADOPTED HIS TWO SONS, AND TOGETHER, THEY HAD A SON, RONNIE, TWO YEARS LATER.

IN 1966, FAMED RECORD PRODUCER PHIL SPECTOR HELPED THE BAND RECORD *RIVER DEEP, MOUNTAIN HIGH*.

THEY TOURED WITH THE ROLLING STONES IN 1969...

...AND, BACKED UP BY THE DANCERS, THE IKETTES, REMADE CREEDENCE CLEARWATER REVIVAL'S "PROUD MARY."

♪♪ I'M THE GYPSY, THE ACID QUEEN! PAY ME BEFORE I START. I'M THE GYPSY, I'M GUARANTEED TO TEAR YOUR SOUL APART! ♪♪

IN 1975, SHE PLAYED THE ACID QUEEN IN THE WHO'S MUSICAL FILM, *TOMMY*.

ONSTAGE AND IN FRONT OF THE MEDIA, THEY WERE A POWERHOUSE COUPLE. BUT BEHIND THE SCENES?

IKE DESCRIBED THEIR TIME TOGETHER LIKE THIS:

"WHEN I MET HER, SHE WAS ANNA MAE. I WAS THE ONE WHO TURNED HER INTO TINA TURNER.

YOU'RE NOT EVEN TRYIN' TO MAKE HIT RECORDS. YOU KNOW THAT! WHAT'S THE MATTER WITH YOU?

"I HAD TO TELL HER HOW TO DRESS, HOW TO WALK, AND HOW TO TALK ON STAGE. I TOLD HER HOW TO STAND AND HOW TO LOOK, THE WHOLE THING, MAN, I MEAN FROM THE WIG DOWN.

NOW PULL YOURSELF TOGETHER! YOU'RE ON IN A MINUTE. DAMN.

"IN THOSE DAYS, MAN, IN THE '50S, BLACK PEOPLE IN THE SOUTH... WE DIDN'T RECOGNIZE CONTRACTS THAT MUCH. AND WE DIDN'T RECOGNIZE MARRIAGES THAT MUCH, EITHER.

"I'M NOT GONNA TRY TO DEFEND OR UNDO WHAT'S BEEN DONE. ALL I COULD SAY ABOUT WHATEVER'S BEEN DONE, IT'S BEEN DONE, AND IT'S WATER UNDER THE BRIDGE. I HAVE NO REGRETS ABOUT MY LIFE.

"I BELIEVE I WAS AHEAD OF MY TIME."

WHEN TINA LEFT IKE, SHE HAD 36 CENTS AND A MOBIL GAS CREDIT CARD. SHE TOOK ON THE DEBTS INCURRED BECAUSE OF THE DIVORCE, INCLUDING PENALTIES FOR CANCELED GIGS AND UNPAID TAXES.

SHE REFUSED TO ASK FOR SPOUSAL SUPPORT OR ROYALTIES FOR THEIR MUSIC - THINGS SHE WAS ENTITLED TO RECEIVE. SHE ONLY DEMANDED ONE THING:

SHE WANTED TO KEEP THE NAME TINA TURNER. SHE WASN'T GOING TO GIVE UP HER DREAM.

"MY LEGACY IS THAT I STAYED ON COURSE - FROM THE BEGINNING TO THE END - BECAUSE I BELIEVED IN SOMETHING INSIDE OF ME," SHE TOLD AN INTERVIEWER.

HER STAR DIMMED, SHE PLAYED CABARET SHOWS AT CAESAR'S PALACE IN LAS VEGAS,

APPEARED ON TELEVISION IN *THE HOLLYWOOD SQUARES*,

AND *THE SONNY & CHER SHOW*.

TINA ALWAYS BELIEVED SHE COULD MAKE A SUCCESSFUL COMEBACK. HER FIRST TWO ALBUMS, "ROUGH" AND "LOVE EXPLOSION," FAILED TO CHART.

AN APPEARANCE ON *OLIVIA NEWTON-JOHN: HOLLYWOOD NIGHTS* IN 1980 WOULD CHANGE EVERYTHING.

FILMED IN LATE 1979, *HOLLYWOOD NIGHTS* INTRODUCED TINA TO LEE KRAMER, NEWTON-JOHN'S MANAGER, AND A YOUNG MAN WORKING FOR HIM, A FRESH-FACED 27-YEAR-OLD AUSTRALIAN NAME ROGER DAVIES.

IN FEBRUARY OF 1980, ROGER AND HIS EMPLOYER, KRAMER, SAW TINA PERFORM IN THE VENETIAN ROOM AT THE FAIRMONT HOTEL IN SAN FRANCISCO.

THE FAIRMONT WAS A CELEBRITY MAGNET, ATTRACTING LOU RAWLS, TONY BENNETT, JACK JONES, RICH LITTLE, VIKKI CARR, AND MORE. OVER THE YEARS, IT WAS KNOWN AS THE "GRANDE DAME," "DEMOCRATIC CENTRAL," AND THE "BORDELLO ON THE HILL."

SHE OPENED WITH A COVER OF ELTON JOHN'S "THE BITCH IS BACK"

AND ENDED WITH "PROUD MARY."

♪♪ I ENTERTAIN BY PICKING BRAINS SELL MY SOUL BY DROPPING NAMES... ♪♪

DURING A BREAK, TINA TOLD ROGER AND LEE:

I WANT TO GET OUT OF HERE AND PLAY ROCK VENUES.

ROGER IMMEDIATELY PUT HER ON TOUR - A FIVE-WEEK GIG OF SOUTH AFRICA.

A SECOND TOUR FOLLOWED IN THE FAR EAST AND AUSTRALIA. BUT SOMETHING SEEMED OFF. ALTHOUGH FINANCIALLY VIABLE, ROGER FELT THE SHOWS WERE REHASHES OF HER CABARET ACT. THEY HAD TO THINK BIGGER.

AT A HOTEL IN BANGKOK, ROGER TOLD HER HIS PLAN:

LISTEN, TINA, IF WE'RE EVER GOING TO CHANGE THIS ACT, WE'VE GOT TO CHANGE EVERYTHING. EVERYTHING - THE BAND - THE DANCERS. WHAT YOU NEED IS SOME YOUNG MUSICIANS WITH LOTS OF ENERGY.

YOU NEED TO PLAY MORE ROCK AND ROLL.

OKAY. I'LL DO IT.

TINA SAID IN AN INTERVIEW, "SOMETIMES, YOU'VE GOT TO LET EVERYTHING GO - PURGE YOURSELF. IF YOU ARE UNHAPPY WITH ANYTHING - WHATEVER IS BRINGING YOU DOWN - GET RID OF IT. BECAUSE YOU'LL FIND THAT WHEN YOU'RE FREE, YOUR TRUE CREATIVITY, YOUR TRUE SELF COMES OUT."

A COVER OF AL GREEN'S "LET'S STAY TOGETHER" HIT #6 IN THE U.K. CAPITAL RECORDS, SEEING THE SONG'S SUCCESS AS IT MADE ITS WAY THROUGH CLUBS IN THE STATES, RELEASED THE SINGLE.

A STRING OF HITS FOLLOWED.

♪♪ I'M YOUR PRIVATE DANCER, A DANCER FOR MONEY. I'LL DO WHAT YOU WANT ME TO DO. ♪♪

SHE APPEARED IN MOVIES...

WELCOME TO ANOTHER EDITION OF THUNDERDOME!

AND, IN 1990, SHE PLAYED OVER 125 SHOWS FOR 3.5 MILLION PEOPLE IN HER EUROPEAN TOUR. SHE'D CONTINUE TO TOUR OFF AND ON FOR SEVERAL MORE YEARS. TINA TURNER WAS REBORN.

IN 1991, IKE AND TINA TURNER WERE INDUCTED INTO THE ROCK AND ROLL HALL OF FAME. IN 2021, TINA WAS INDUCTED AGAIN – THIS TIME AS A SOLO ACT.

IN 1993, A MOVIE WAS MADE ABOUT HER LIFE. THE INDOMITABLE ANGELA BASSETT PLAYED TINA.

TINA: THE TINA TURNER MUSICAL PREMIERED ON APRIL 17, 2018. FOR TWO HOURS AND FORTY-FIVE MINUTES, THEATRE-GOERS ARE TREATED TO A ROTATION OF HER GREATEST HITS, NEW SONGS, AND A DRAMATIZATION OF HER LIFE.

HBO'S BIOPIC, TINA, RELEASED MARCH 27, 2021, FEELS LIKE HER SWAN SONG.

"SOME PEOPLE SAY THE LIFE THAT I'VE LIVED AND THE PERFORMANCES I GAVE...THE APPRECIATION IS LASTING WITH THE PEOPLE, AND I SHOULD BE PROUD OF THAT," TURNER SAID IN AN INTERVIEW.

"I AM. BUT WHEN DO YOU STOP BEING PROUD? HOW DO YOU BOW OUT SLOWLY – JUST GO AWAY?"

ALTHOUGH TINA MAY "GO AWAY," HER LEGACY ENDURES.

"I NEVER FELT SORRY FOR MYSELF. ONCE YOU START THE SELF-PITY, YOU'RE DEAD – YOU'RE IN THE BOX. I DIDN'T ALLOW MYSELF TO GO IN THAT FRIGGIN' BOX. THAT'S THE MESSAGE. DON'T ACCEPT IT. KEEP GOING."

Michael Frizell ⸺⸺⸺⸺⸺ Writer

Ramon Salas ⸺⸺⸺⸺⸺ Art

Benjamin Glibert ⸺⸺⸺⸺ Letters

Darren G. Davis ⸺⸺⸺⸺ Editor

Ramon Salas ⸺⸺⸺⸺⸺ Cover

Cover B: Joe Phillips

Darren G. Davis
Publisher

Maggie Jessup
Publicity

Susan Ferris
Entertainment Manager

Steven Diggs Jr.
Marketing Manager

CPSIA information can be obtained
at www.ICGtesting.com
Printed in the USA
BVHW051742241121
622381BV00004B/43